JOSCA AILINE BAROUKH
CAMILA SAMPAIO

LET'S TAKE A BATH

TRANSLATION BY
NATHAN BAROUKH • LILIANA CASTRO

Text © Josca Ailine Baroukh
Illustration © Camila Sampaio

Editorial Director
Marcelo Duarte

Book Design
Vanessa Sayuri Sawada

Commercial Director
Patth Pachas

Printing
PifferPrint

Special Projects Director
Tatiana Fulas

Editorial Coordinator
Vanessa Sayuri Sawada

Editorial Assistants
Camila Martins
Henrique Torres

CIP-BRASIL. CATALOGAÇÃO NA PUBLICAÇÃO
SINDICATO NACIONAL DOS EDITORES DE LIVROS, RJ

B246L
Baroukh, Josca Ailine
Let's take a bath / Josca Ailine Baroukh, Camila Sampaio; tradução Nathan Baroukh, Liliana Castro. – 1. ed. – São Paulo: Panda Books, 2022. 24 pp. il.

Tradução de: Vamos tomar banho?
ISBN 978-65-5697-139-1

1. Ficção. 2. Literatura infantojuvenil brasileira. I. Sampaio, Camila. II. Baroukh, Nathan. III. Castro, Liliana. IV. Título.

21-72634
CDD: 808.899282
CDU: 82-93(81)

Bibliotecária: Meri Gleice Rodrigues de Souza – CRB-7/6439

2022
All rights reserved to Panda Books.
A division of Editora Original Ltda.
R. Henrique Schaumann, 286, cj. 41
05413-010 – São Paulo – SP – Brazil
Tel./Fax: 55 (11) 3088-8444
edoriginal@pandabooks.com.br
www.pandabooks.com.br
Visit us on Facebook, Instagram and Twitter.

No part of this publication may be reproduced, distributed, or transmitted, in any form or by any means without the prior authorization of Editora Original Ltda. Copyright infringement is established in Law number 9.610/98 and punished by article 184 of the Brazilian Criminal Code.

WATER IN A BASIN, A BUCKET, OR THE SINK! SPRINKLER IN THE LAWN, HOW FUN!...

HOW ABOUT YOU?
WHERE DO YOU LIKE
TO TAKE A BATH?

JOSCA AILINE BAROUKH

Despite my complicated name, I was born in São Paulo, Brazil. With a name like that, it was expected me to get a nickname: even today everyone calls me Jo.

I always enjoyed playing in the water – a bath, in the rain, in the waterfall. Since I was little, I've loved to swim in the ocean. At first, on my father's lap; little by little, I gained the confidence to jump waves alone, in the shallow. When I learned to swim, I would swim in the sea and in the pool.

I studied psychology and soon realized that I wanted to be a teacher. Today, I do what I like best: I visit schools, talk with children and teachers about the importance of watching, listening, and playing with little ones.

CAMILA SAMPAIO

I was born in Minas Gerais, and today I live in São Paulo, with my husband and two kittens, Pingo and Gigi. I have fun watching them cleaning themselves, licking their little feet, their belly... And sometimes they even clean each other! But a cat bath is very different from ours... They can't stand the shower!

I love to draw and to take a shower. Once I was on a trip and found little markers for drawing on glass and tiles. They have an ink that washes off with water, and I finally figured out a way to do both at the same time! Now I just need to find a waterproof book, and I won't have any reason to get out of the shower, ever. I think I should turn into a mermaid!